MORNING *Tea*

VOLUME 1

DAILY ENCOURAGEMENTS FOR ENTREPRENEURS

BY RACHEL JENKS

Copyright © 2021 by Rachel Jenks

All rights reserved, including the right to reproduce this book or portions thereof in any form whatsoever or by any means. No part of this book may be reproduced, stored in a retrieval system, or transmitted by any means without the written permission of the Author, except as provided by United States of America copyright law.

First Paperback edition August 2021

Manufactured in the United States of America

Scriptures referred to in this book are taken from the most up to date translations of the Holy Bible published by Zondervan Publishing House and provided online by Biblegateway.com.

Morning Tea Brand and Cover Design by The Brand Boss Studio Copyright © 2021.

Strategic Design Boss: Melissa Buck

Published by Victory Vision Publishing and Consulting, LLC
victoryvision.org

ISBN: **9798458733762**

Dedication

This book is dedicated to you, the reader.

May the words that have so strengthened me, now embolden and encourage you.

Contents

Acknowledgments	i	Truth Nugget #17	p97
Introduction	iii	Truth Nugget #18	p103
Truth Nugget #1	p1	Truth Nugget #19	p109
Truth Nugget #2	p7	Truth Nugget #20	p115
Truth Nugget #3	p13	Truth Nugget #21	p121
Truth Nugget #4	p19	Truth Nugget #22	p127
Truth Nugget #5	p25	Truth Nugget #23	p133
Truth Nugget #6	p31	Truth Nugget #24	p139
Truth Nugget #7	p37	Truth Nugget #25	p145
Truth Nugget #8	p43	Truth Nugget #26	p151
Truth Nugget #9	p49	Truth Nugget #27	p157
Truth Nugget #10	p55	Truth Nugget #28	p163
Truth Nugget #11	p61	Truth Nugget #29	p169
Truth Nugget #12	p67	Truth Nugget #30	p175
Truth Nugget #13	p73	Truth Nugget #31	p181
Truth Nugget #14	p79	About the Author	p187
Truth Nugget #15	p85	More on Morning Tea	p188
Truth Nugget #16	p91	Resources	p189

Acknowledgements

To my favorite tea date of all time. I cannot begin to put into words my gratitude for who You are. You are my Daddy. My Best Friend. And the best Business Advisor. Life with You is my favorite adventure.

To Carl and Susi Jenks – the ones who taught me to listen for His voice, trust that I hear Him, and who have championed me in my journey of pursuing what He says. Thank you for being you, and for your lifestyle of connection with Him, and each other, that inspired Morning Tea. I love you so much!!

To Stephen and Veronica Jenks – My Dude and Sis. Thank you for loving me so well through every step of this journey…every milestone and every mile. I love you!!

To my Abigail – My darling niece, may your ear always be tuned to His voice. I know you hear Him even now. You are the greatest joy of my life, and I eagerly look forward to our conversations about what He's speaking to you!

To my Wonder – It's here!! The first of many. Thank you for singing my song, always reminding me of every single one of His promises. With planting comes harvest, and I cannot wait to celebrate with YOU!!

To my TT – How do I begin to thank you for who you are? You have stood with me, wept with me, rejoiced with me, dreamed with me, walked with me, and even fed me on this journey. Thank you for tangibly modeling for me what unconditional love looks like.

To Friend – As they say, "we've come a long way, baby," haven't we?! Who would have thought we'd be on the journeys we're on now. So grateful we get to do life together and keep cheering each other on, even across the miles. I am truly a #proudfriend. I love you!!

To Julie – THANK YOU for bringing victory to this vision!! I am so grateful for you and honor who you are!

And to the Morning Tea community – thank you for the honor of sharing with you from my journey, and moreover, from His heart. I am deeply grateful for each of you!

To everyone who has encouraged me, prayed for me, stood with me, and cheered me on...Thank you!!

Introduction

~~~~~~~

**Welcome to Volume 1 of Morning Tea:
Daily Encouragements for Entrepreneurs!**

I'm so honored to meet you!

I'm Rachel, and this is my journal.

It was the summer of 2017. My fledgling business was a little over a year old. I was sitting on the couch one morning when I had the thought, "I don't want You just to be my business partner."

You see, I've been blessed to be on this adventure of life with God for a long time; thirty-eight years, at the time of this writing. I grew up knowing Jesus as my Best Friend... not as something I learned in Sunday School, but as my constant companion, friend, and confidante in all of life's adventures. Like Samuel in the Bible, my ear has been tuned to the voice of the Lord since I was a young child, and our conversations are rich and ongoing.

When I launched full-time into the world of entrepreneurship in 2016, it was because, and only because... He said it was time. In the natural it made no sense. I wish I could tell you I had money saved up and a roster of clients in the wings... but none of that was the case. I launched the night my department at work had been eliminated due to budget cuts. I was in the middle of a serious health scare, and in many ways, it felt like everything in my life was swirling. But that night, through my tears, I heard Him say, "It's time." And I decided a long time ago that He has my yes.

And so I launched, on the homemade laptop my friend built for me because I didn't even have a computer... (shout out to KJ and Emily!!) that even now, 5 years later, I am using to scribe this book.

My entrepreneurial journey has been a wild one, with adventures I could never have dreamed up even if I tried – and I have a pretty vivid imagination! And every step of the way, He's held me, guided me, and yes, even pushed me out of the nest when I needed it! It's our conversations that have directed me, sustained me, and kept me going when all I wanted to do was throw in the towel and give up. But that's a story for another book! *wink*

So there I was, on my red couch that July 2017 morning, having a conversation. We were talking about my business, as we usually do in the mornings... and suddenly I realized that had become all we were talking about. And I was doing most of the talking.

I thought of couples who intentionally choose connection rather than letting their relationship get swallowed up in everyday busyness. I thought of my parents. They wear many hats and have partnered together powerfully in ministry, life, and even business. And every morning, as long as I can remember, they have coffee. I don't just mean they drink it... I mean it's an event. My dad (who I call Papa Bear) makes my Mama her coffee and brings it to her... and they sit and enjoy it together. It's more than coffee, it's connection. And whether it was my brother and I, or my dad's early morning elders' meetings... everyone knew "coffee" is do-not-disturb time for my parents to connect and just enjoy being together. There's something so special and so powerful about that.

And as a grin danced across my face, an idea popped in my head... "I want to do that with You!" Personally, I don't care for coffee, but tea is my jam. And in that moment, I decided that God and I now had a tea date every morning.

The very next morning, I made my tea, got cozy on my couch, and...now what? Should I pray? Read my Bible? Worship? What does having tea with God look like? What would He like most?

And clear as day, I heard my Heavenly Daddy say with a smile, "I just want to have tea with you."

And thus began my most treasured, do-not-disturb, daily appointment.

Yes, we do talk business. Some powerful transformation

has happened there on my red couch in between sips. And it is a two-way conversation. But mostly, I listen and journal what He's speaking to me.

When I first started journaling my tea dates, I never in a million years thought anyone else would be reading these. I nearly fell over when one morning, during our tea date, He told me this was my first book! WHAT?! "Um, but this is my journal, God. This is deeply personal." "I know, Honey. Remember when you started? How scared and alone you felt? There are others on the journey who need this. Will you share it?"

And so, dear reader, this... and the volumes to follow... these pages from my journey are my gift to you.

You are not here by accident. I believe it is no coincidence that you are right now holding this book.

So go ahead, pour yourself a fresh cup of tea, or coffee, or whatever your favorite beverage might be...

Get cozy...

And listen...

Because the same One I have tea with every morning has some amazing Tea Time Truth Nuggets to share with you, too.

I can't wait to see what He shows you!

Author's note: This book is designed to be savored like a good cup of tea, one sip at a time. Feel free to make this book part of your morning, or ask Him to highlight which Tea Time Truth Nugget is the one for you today!

Want to start your day with me sharing fresh Tea Time Truth Nuggets live?

Join the Morning Tea community at
https://www.facebook.com/groups/morningtea

*Tea Time
Truth Nugget #1*

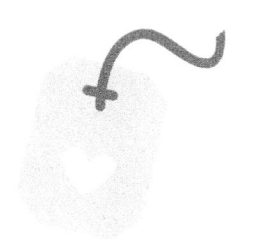

No more hiding. **None.** That is exactly what I want you to leave behind.

You are uniquely created, but you feel like unique is a word that people use like a polite way of saying you don't measure up.

I am telling you that you don't measure up;
you exceed the measure.

Honey, when I made you, I made you to be on display.
I didn't make you to be hidden.

There is beauty in you that all the world is waiting
for you to unveil.

Don't be afraid. I'm calling you out.
It is not beyond you. It is you.

Let it out. Unveil the beauty that you are.
I have been waiting for this moment with bated breath.

You know that moment when Cinderella enters the ball
and is so beautiful that the crowd goes silent?

That moment takes your breath away. And yet every time,
I hear that sigh within you that says,

"I wish I could be that beautiful."

But the truth that you don't see yet is that her dress, her beauty, pales in the light of you.

Can you hear it? Can you truly hear it?

The crowd goes silent when you enter the room. Not when your makeup or clothes or curled hair enter the room. When *you* enter the room. I am telling you, the crowd goes silent. All of Heaven stops and stares.

So will you trust Me? Will you let it out? Will you come out of hiding so I can show you off to the world?

Because that's who I say you are. You are My beauty on display. And I want you to see it, too.

Your Turn!

(Author's note: John 10 says that you are His sheep, and His promise is that you DO hear Him! So don't overthink this. Just ask,...and listen. As my dear friend and mentor Dubb Alexander says, "Maybe it's you, but it's probably God!" And you have permission to practice. The first thing that comes to your mind is probably what He wants you to know!)

Lord, what are You saying to me today? What do You want me to hear from Your heart?

Tea Time

Truth Nugget #2

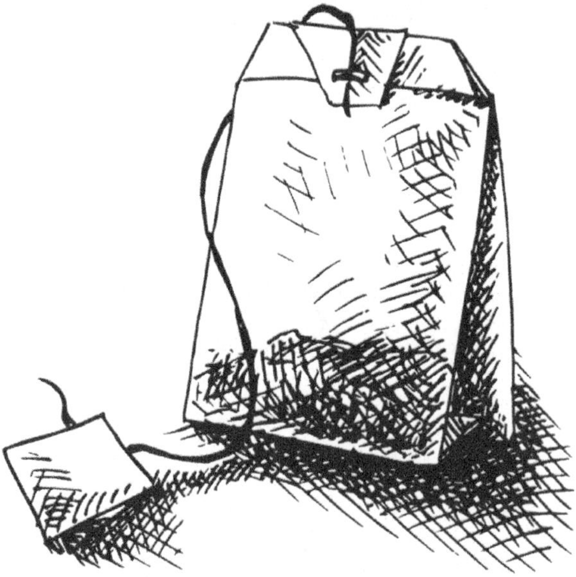

I just want to have tea with you.

I love this ride.

I love this ride because you're on it.

I love how you trust Me.

Bold Faith. Honey.

That's who you are.

Bold faith and joyful hope; it's not one or the other.

You are both.

You are Bold Faith. You are.

And I love how you trust Me.

I love how you put your hands up and just say,

"Okay Daddy, let's go!"

That thrills Me.

You thrill Me.

Life with you is My favorite adventure.

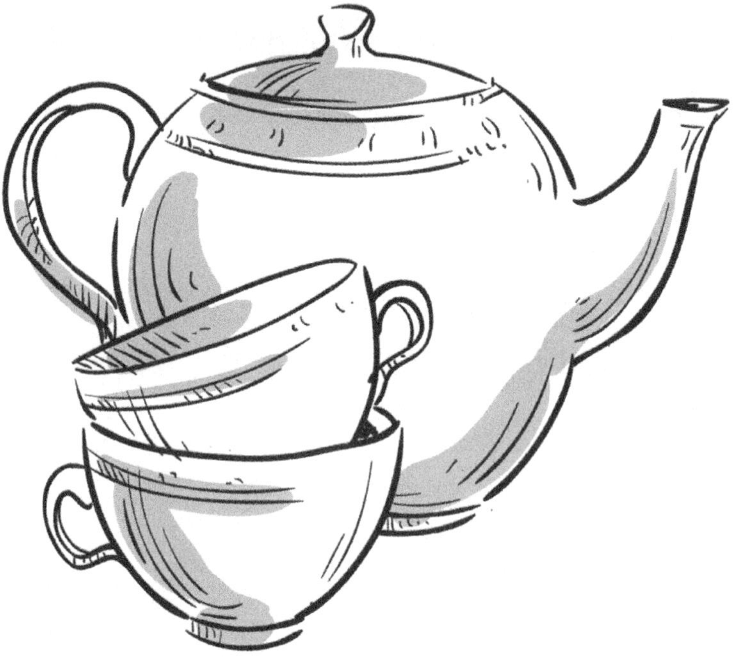

Lord, what are You saying to me today? What do You want me to hear from Your heart?

Tea Time

Truth Nugget #3

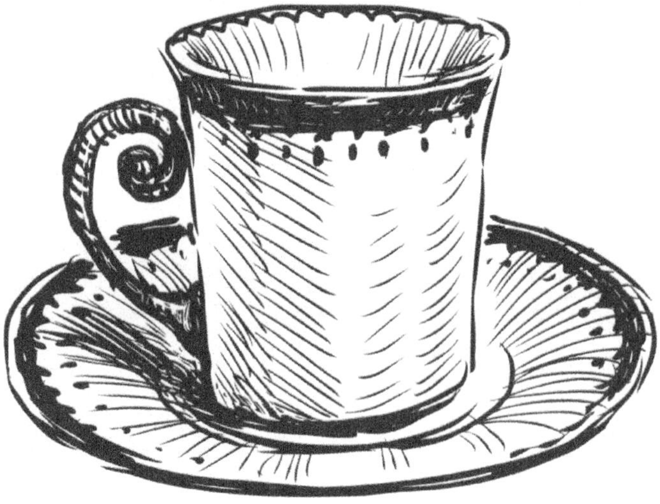

I love you, Honey.

I really love you.

Do you know that?

I mean, do you really know it?

It's the number one limiting belief holding you back right now.

And it's based entirely on the past, which shapes your perception of Me.

I don't want that for you anymore.

It's time to stop looking backwards.

I know it's "hard to jump up and down with a broken foot," but that's not you anymore.

You're not broken.

Do you hear me Honey? You are not broken anymore.

I didn't just fix you. I healed you.

When you read the past into the future, all you see is failure, and that is not the story I'm writing.

This is about freedom.

I want you free, and to get where I'm taking you, I need you to be free.

Those mentors you look up to? They weren't always free.

Those people all around that you think have it so much more together than you do? They're on a journey, too.

Rest in Me.

Rest in my love.

Let's let go of the past, and believe that I really,

really love you...

...and that you have nothing to prove, nothing to hide, and nothing to fear.

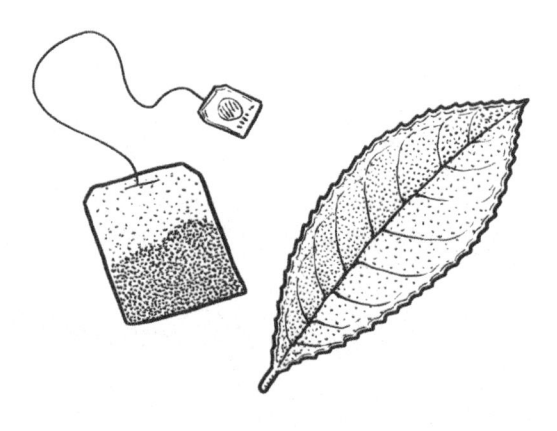

Lord, what are You saying to me today? What do You want me to hear from Your heart?

Tea Time

Truth Nugget #4

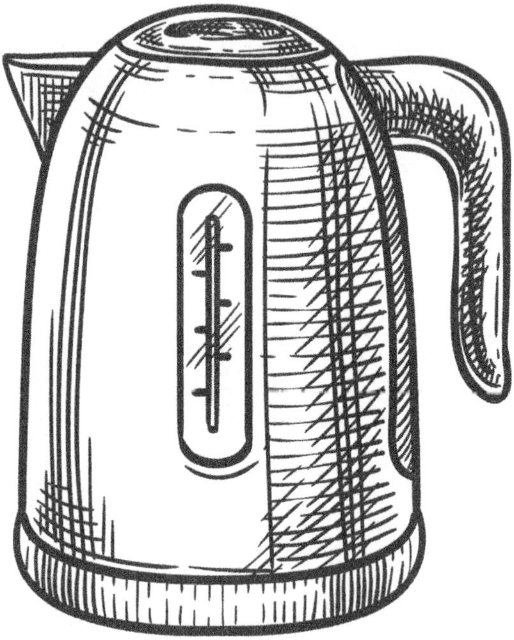

Do you know who you are?

Do you know the value of the role that you play?

I'm about to show you.

So don't freak out, don't be surprised, and don't be afraid.

Cinderella is coming to the ball.

And while she came alone, she didn't end up that way.

Oh Honey, if you knew.

If you only knew the value of the role I have for you to play.

I've been waiting a long time for you.

They have too.

You don't know it yet. You don't see fully, but you will.

I will show you.

But hear Me on this. This is so, so crucial.

I need you not to hide.

I need you not to hide. Not even behind the wall of your own self-perceptions.

This isn't about who you think you are.

This is about who I say you are.

And I'm going to show you.

We're going to have so many adventures. Don't you fret about that.

But it's time for this adventure right now.

Everything you've been seeing, feeling, learning—it's all about this moment, this precipice.

And the view on the other side is

stunningly beautiful.

Don't try to figure it out, you couldn't even if you tried.

Just trust Me.

And please, Honey, don't hide.

Lord, what are You saying to me today? What do You want me to hear from Your heart?

*Tea Time
Truth Nugget #5*

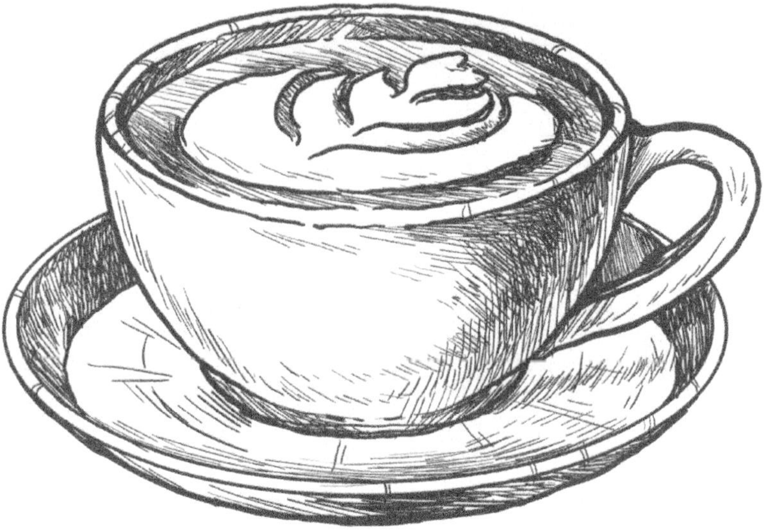

I love having tea with you.

It's My favorite part of the day now.

Do you know that?

I love it all. But tea; yeah, that's My favorite part.

Just being, and talking,...

And I get to tell you how much I love you.

It's okay, Honey, it is really okay.

I got this.

Everything that you don't know how it's going to get done, or you don't yet see how it's going to be accomplished...

I got this.

I'm positioning you for growth.

It is time for upgrade.

I have bigger places for you than you know.

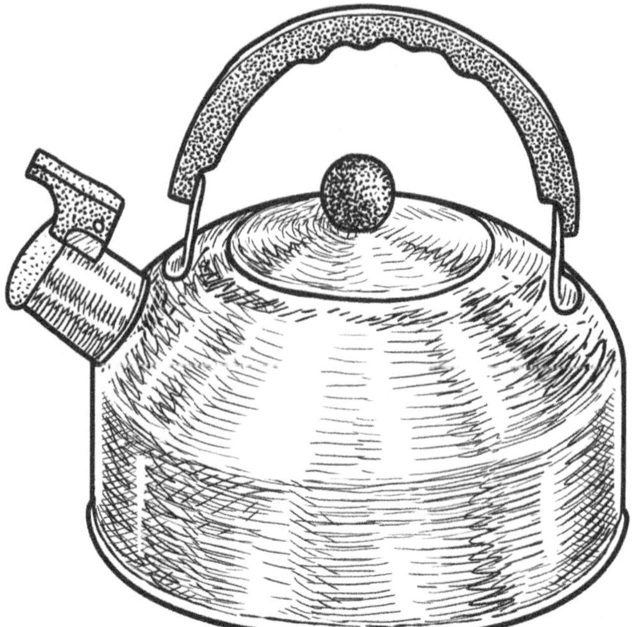

Lord, what are You saying to me today? What do You want me to hear from Your heart?

*Tea Time
Truth Nugget #6*

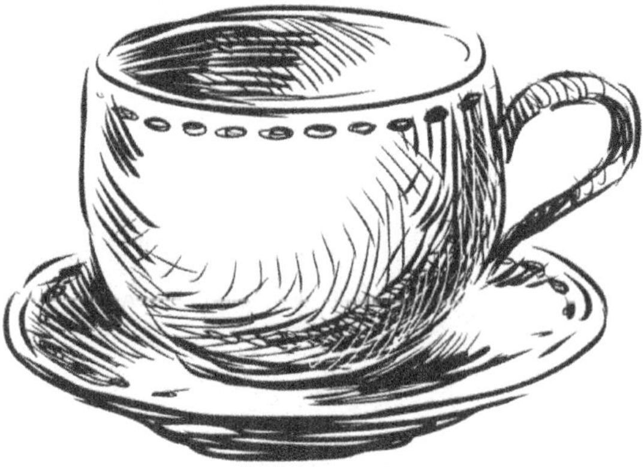

We're going places, you and I.

I have people in places and in positions of authority that need what you have.

And, they need to know you have it.

They need encouragement. They need answers.

They need hope. They need joy.

They need Me. They need you.

You're impacting the atmosphere.

You want clients; I have them.

You want your team; I have them too—ALL of them.

It's coming.

It's all coming.

But I need to know if you will go.

Don't rush. Don't get anxious.

I've got this...all of this.

Know that, Honey.

Know that I've got this, and know that it is coming.

All of it.

Will you go?

Lord, what are You saying to me today? What do You want me to hear from Your heart?

Tea Time

Truth Nugget #7

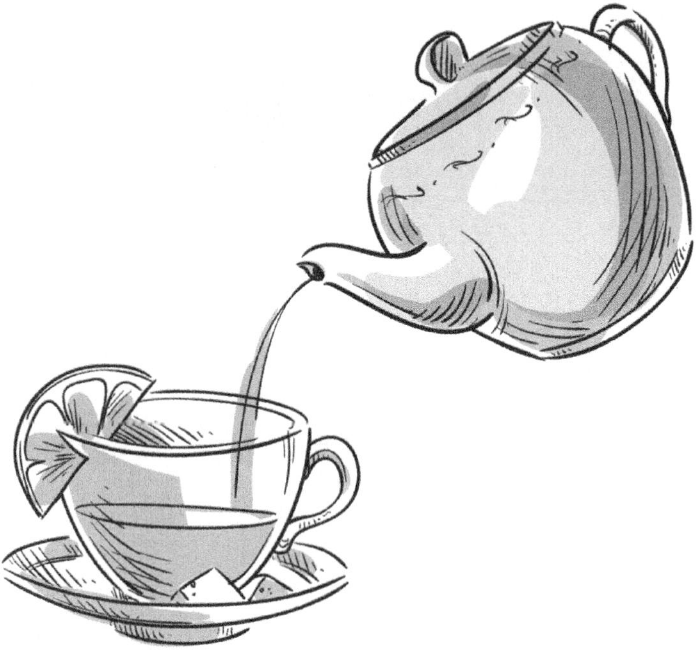

Hey.

Here I am.

I never went anywhere.

Take a deep breath, Honey.

It's going to be okay.

There's time for it; for all of it.

I have time, and I always have time for people.

It's gonna get busy, Honey, really busy.

But here I am. Here I am in the midst of the busy, and the deadlines and the noise.

Here I am, right here, right now.

And I have a plan, and a strategy, and an agenda.

I am your compass.

You know that, but don't let busy cause you to forget.

Listen.

Wait.

Rest.

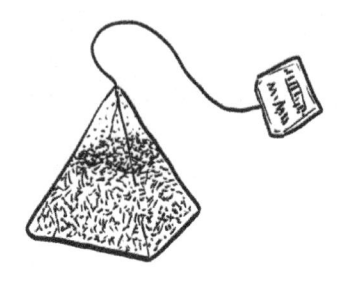

Not a rest of not doing; but a rest of doing differently.

A rest of obedience.

A rest of trust.

A rest of knowing that your Father's got this... all of it.

Now, let's get to work.

Lord, what are You saying to me today? What do You want me to hear from Your heart?

Tea Time

Truth Nugget #8

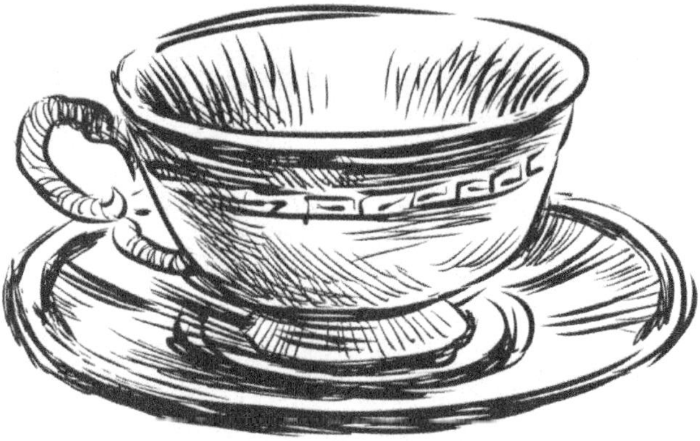

Happy New Day, Honey! Do you hear that?

Happy New Day.

Today is the first day of a new season for you, and it's gonna be good. I'm so proud of you.

Do you know that I am so proud of you?

I love you.

You're afraid to even write it, but...today it begins, all of it, right now.

Let go of the past. Let all the way go. Especially the weight of every failed expectation.

We're writing a new story now, and you can't find any of the scripts looking behind.

It's a new day. Right now, don't be afraid.

I know it's been a long, hard season, and I'm proud of you, so very proud of you. You didn't quit.

You didn't buckle, even when you wanted to.

I know it's hard to hear, and even scarier to write...but listen, Honey. I am saying that right now, today, a new season has begun.

So get ready, because here it comes.

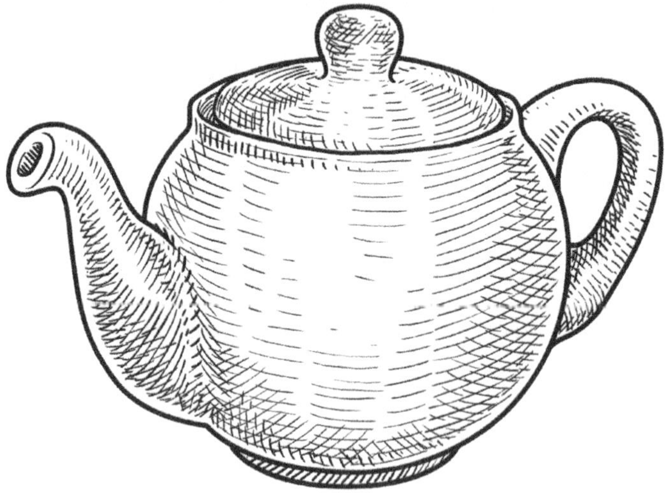

Lord, what are You saying to me today? What do You want me to hear from Your heart?

Tea Time Truth Nugget #9

I love you, Honey.

Are you ready for an adventure?

A really fun adventure?

It's okay.

You're tired.

You don't have to be perfect today.

We're going to do some work today, but we're going to work from rest.

Just rest.

Rest in Me.

I want to bless you more than you can even imagine.

And I will take care of all of the details.

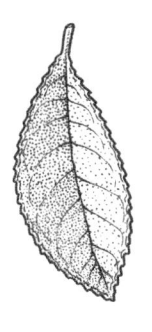

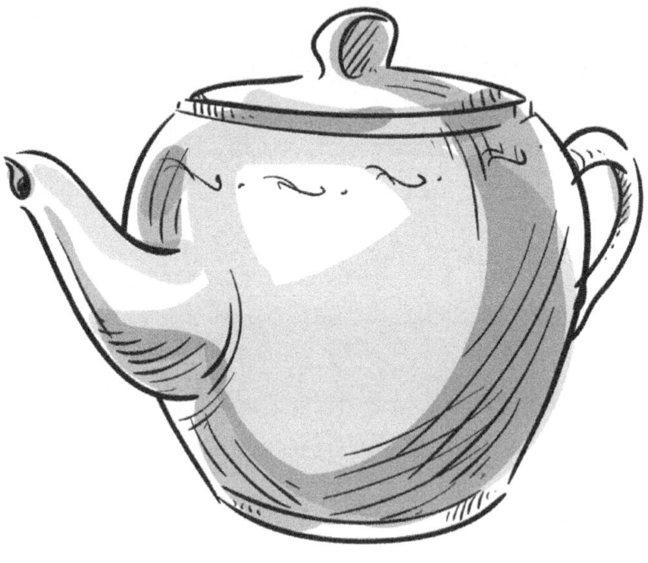

Lord, what are You saying to me today? What do You want me to hear from Your heart?

Tea Time

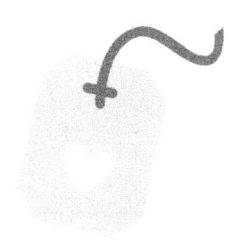

Truth Nugget #10

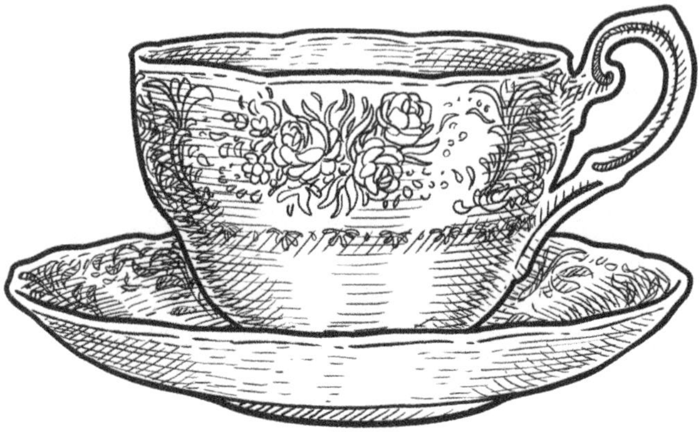

I wasn't kidding.

I told you, Honey, and I wasn't kidding.

This is a new season.

It's all new, all of it.

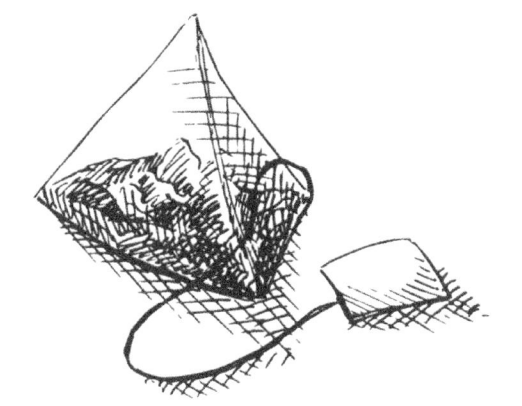

Get ready.

We're going on an adventure.

A really fun adventure.

If you knew what I have up My sleeve, it would scare you, just like all of this does right now.

Which is why I haven't told you yet,

but here it comes!

1 · 2 · 3

We're jumping headlong and headfirst into this new season.

Do or do not, there is no try.

But you're ready.

I made you ready.

I equip the called, and you are ready.

Do you hear Me, Honey? You're ready.

I say you're ready.

So take a deep breath and hang on tight.

You're gonna love this ride.

Lord, what are You saying to me today? What do You want me to hear from Your heart?

Tea Time

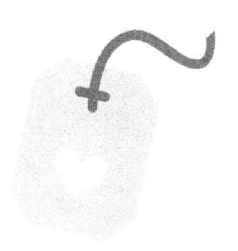

Truth Nugget #11

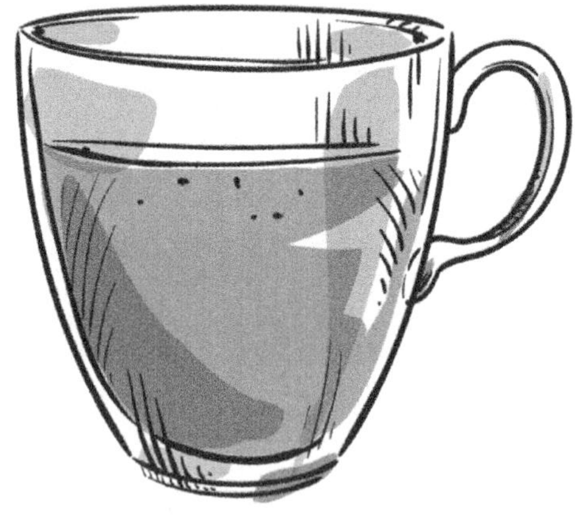

Do you trust Me?

I know all the things you have on your plate right now.

I gave them to you.

And I know how to help you accomplish them.

Here's the thing about business—there will always be more work to do. Always.

There will always be more emails to read and write. The key is learning what to do when.

Because from here on out,
you're going to be busy, very busy.

Which isn't to say there will be no rest.

It's going to be uncomfortable for a little while, because it's time to scale.

But it's okay, Honey. I got this.

I got you.

I have rest for you in the midst of chaos.

And I have the agenda.

You have enough. You have enough time.

Don't worry.

Don't let worry or idleness steal your joy.

Just ask Me for the agenda and follow My lead—not the tyranny of the urgent.

That's very important.

There will always be urgent,

but I will show you what is best.

Lord, what are You saying to me today? What do You want me to hear from Your heart?

Tea Time

Truth Nugget #12

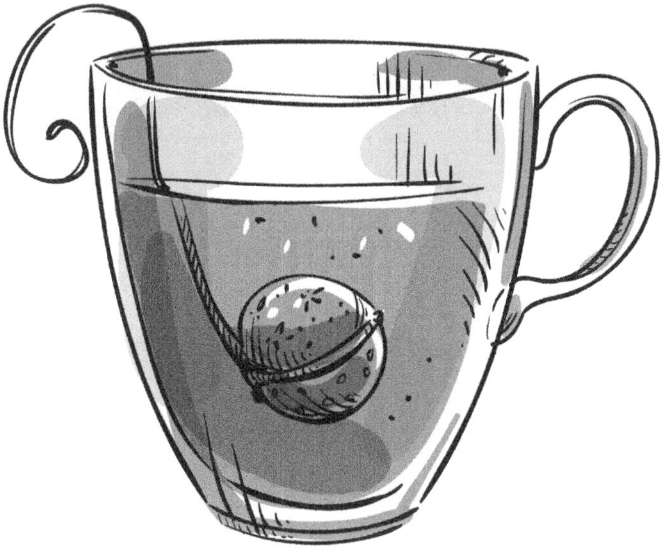

We've only just begun, Honey.

We've only just begun.

Don't be afraid. The joy you feel right now
is not a one-time feeling.

Underline that. It's new, all new.

I am doing a new thing.

Even now it springs forth, do you not perceive it?

It's coming, Honey. It's all coming.

It's going to be so good, and it's all new.

I love lavishing you.

Now, don't do that. Don't compare your journey to anyone else. I didn't give you their journey.

I gave you yours, custom-tailored for you.

There are those around you who need your joy right now.

Don't hide it.

Don't squelch it.

Be you.

Live your journey.

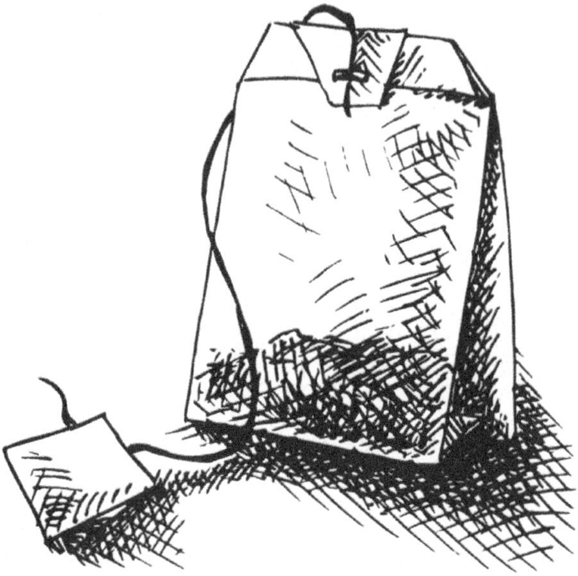

Lord, what are You saying to me today? What do You want me to hear from Your heart?

Tea Time

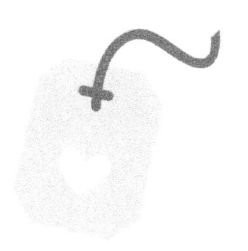

Truth Nugget #13

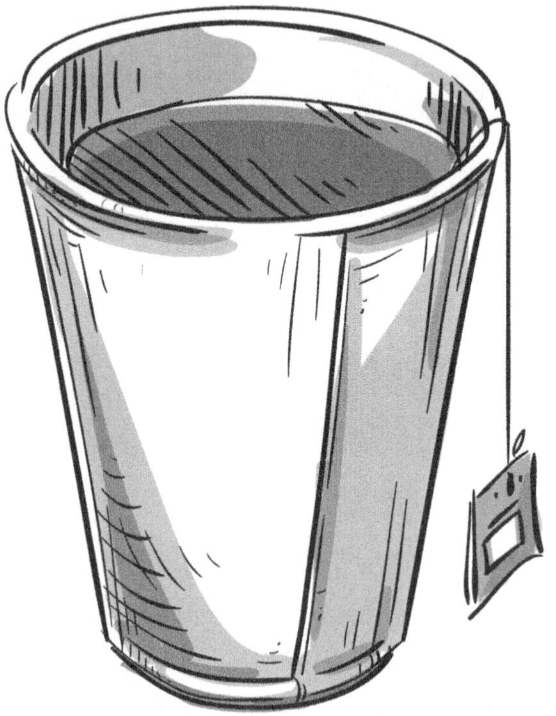

Wisdom lives in you.

Wisdom makes hard decisions sometimes.

And everything that is unfolding in your life right now is setting the stage for more.

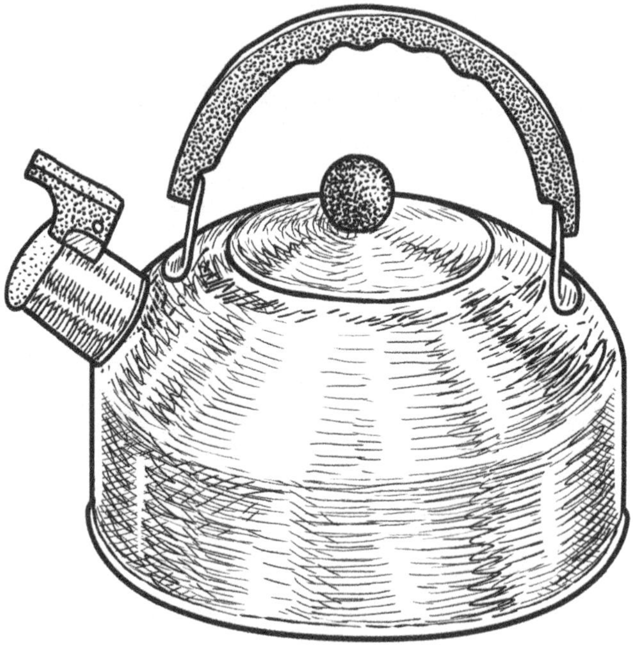

Lord, what are You saying to me today? What do You want me to hear from Your heart?

Tea Time

Truth Nugget #14

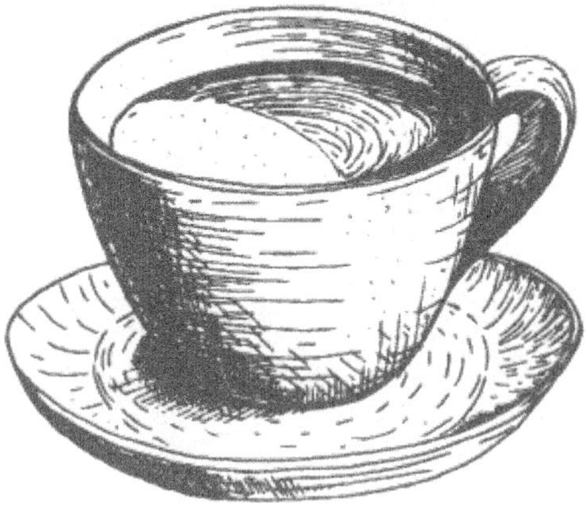

Focus, Honey.

Focus is going to be your word of the day and of the week.

Focus is the key to accomplishing what I have set out for you to do.

And focus is the key to moving forward.

Eyes on Me.

Straight ahead.

Listen for My yes.

Stay focused. One thing at a time, one person at a time. Keep your focus.

People will feel it, people will know it.

You will know it.

Your work will reflect it.

Keep your focus, keep your peace.

Don't get in a rush.

Don't get distracted.

Don't let the needs of others pull you off course.

There are good things, and then there are best.

Let Me set your best.

Keep your focus and it will all get done.

Get distracted = get behind.

But you've got this, Honey.

Learn focus now, and you will have focus later.

Let's get to work.

Lord, what are You saying to me today? What do You want me to hear from Your heart?

*Tea Time
Truth Nugget #15*

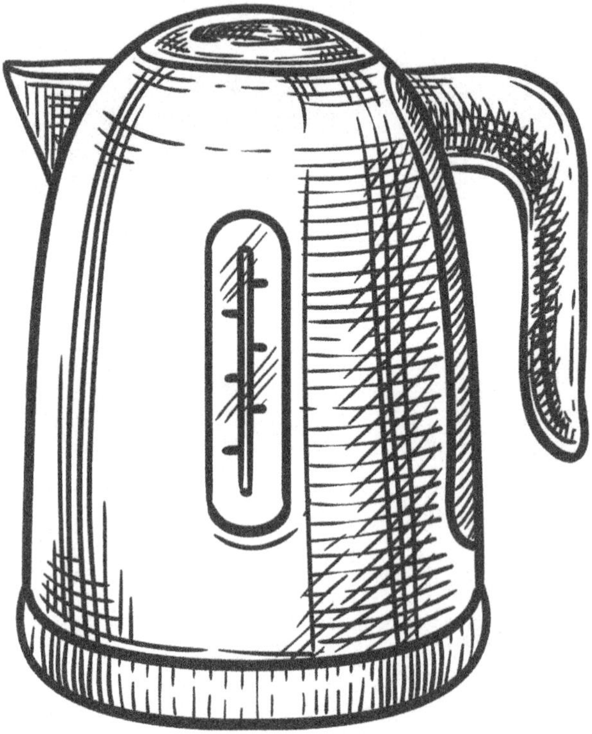

Training time, Honey.

It's training time, and you've entered a whole new level.

Let's talk ballet for a minute.

First you learn plié and tendu...and then jumps and jeté... passé then piqué...

And everything builds on each other.

That's exactly what is happening now.

Everything you've learned this past year is building upon each other.

You're no longer learning how to start a business; you're learning how to run a business.

You're learning how to be a CEO.

Remember, Honey, no more hiding.

The season for hiding is over and done.

And when you come out of hiding, you are seen.

You are seen for the excellence that is you,
it's who you are.

I made you excellent, and that is exactly

why you can't settle.

You're not satisfied with anything less than excellence in you, your team, and your work, and that's a good thing, a very good thing.

And that kind of excellence - gets noticed, stands out, and is in high demand.

Remember, I told you that you will never lack

opportunities.

These are the baby ones.

I know they feel huge now,
but these are the training wheels.

Trust Me.

Here we go!

Lord, what are You saying to me today? What do You want me to hear from Your heart?

Tea Time

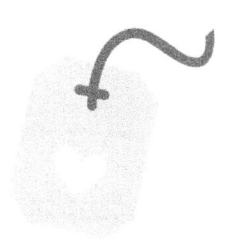

Truth Nugget #16

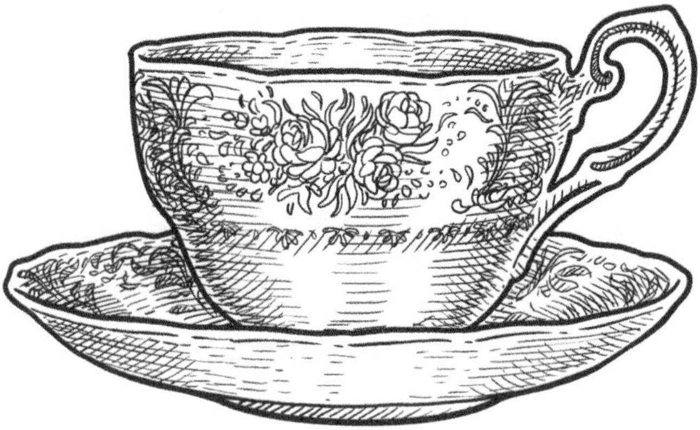

Day of destiny.

Today is a day of destiny.

Things are happening today, and will happen, that have more significance than you know.

Don't run ahead. Wait.

Be here, be in this moment with Me.

I am unfolding you today.

I am unfolding your beauty.

Yes, I said it.

I am unfolding your beauty and your character.

You are going to be noticed today.

So don't be afraid. Get noticed.

No more hiding. None. Not allowed.

Don't be afraid.

Cinderella is going to the ball—not as the servant girl, but as who she really is.

You've been so focused on changing you.

That's what shame does.

Because you start to believe that you are not enough.

But I am breaking off of you that shame mindset and mentality.

You are more than enough.

I am so proud of you, so, so proud.

Let me show you off.

I have places that need to see you, and faces I need you to see.

May I have this dance?

Lord, what are You saying to me today? What do You want me to hear from Your heart?

Tea Time
Truth Nugget #17

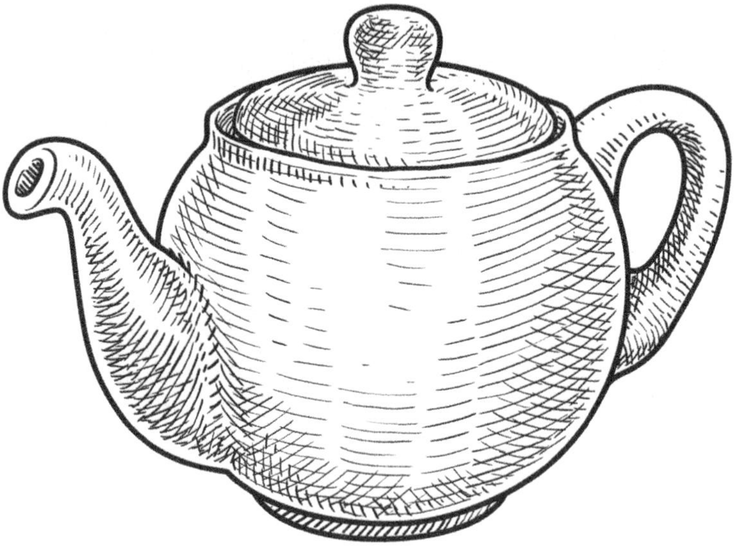

It's just the beginning.

Get comfortable.

You've been so comfortable with failure that you've come to expect it.

Get comfortable with success.

You're no longer a slave to fear in your mind.

And because of your mind, it's going to be very important that you don't look around...

Not at any of the entrepreneurs around you, not at your mentors...

Your path is not going to look like theirs.

I have you on a different trajectory - Mine.

You've been living in scarcity again, time, money, food, showers, even people.

You've been living like there's not enough...

Like you're not enough...

And that's just plain not true. It's okay, Honey. It's okay.

You're learning, and We are going to get there.

We are. Together.

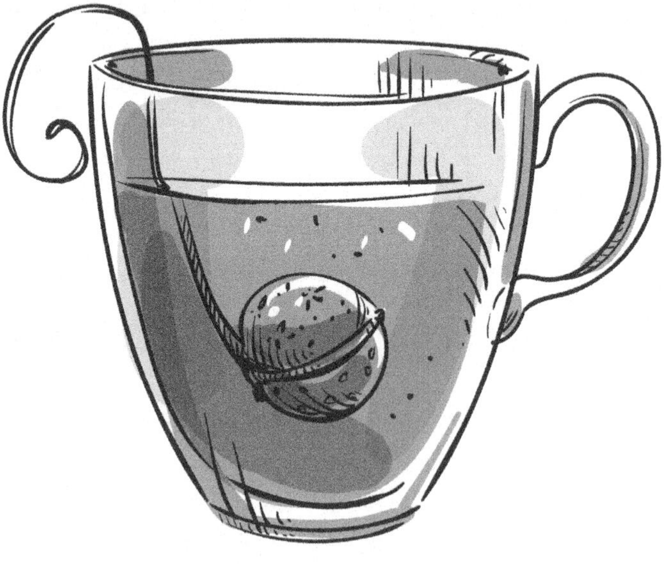

Lord, what are You saying to me today? What do You want me to hear from Your heart?

Tea Time

Truth Nugget #18

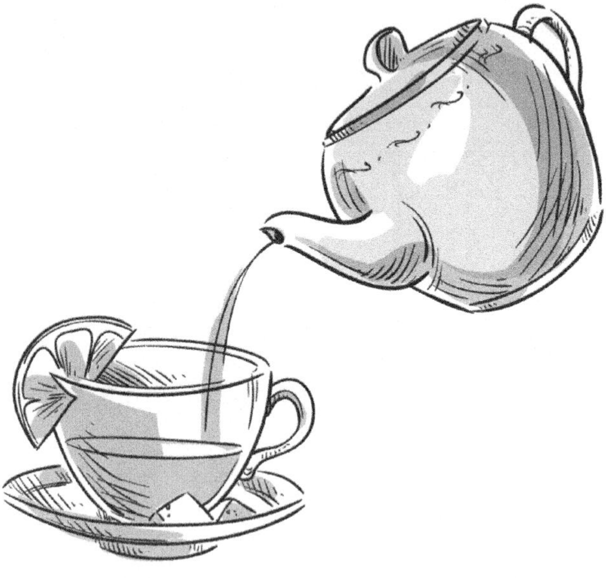

Let's do this. Honey, let's really do this.

Jump in.

Don't be afraid to get your feet wet and your clothes dirty.

You've been tiptoeing to the edge... excited but scared, nervous, unsure, timid...

Jump!

It is going to be a good adventure.

The water might be very cold and fast. The hike might be steep, but you can do it.

I'm saying you can.

Now is not the time to look down, it's the time to look up - way up, because that's where you're going.

You don't think you can get there, but I know you can.

It is okay.

Get your bearings. Catch your breath.

Let others carry your pack when you need to.

We're going up — all the way up.

Not just partway, not just some of the way, all the way.

That high peak was just the beginning.

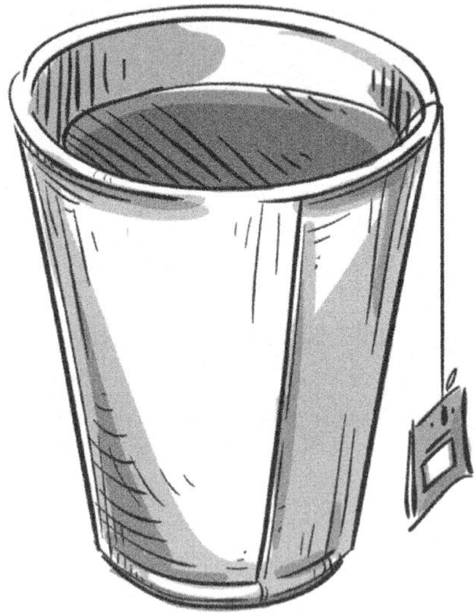

Lord, what are You saying to me today? What do You want me to hear from Your heart?

Tea Time

Truth Nugget #19

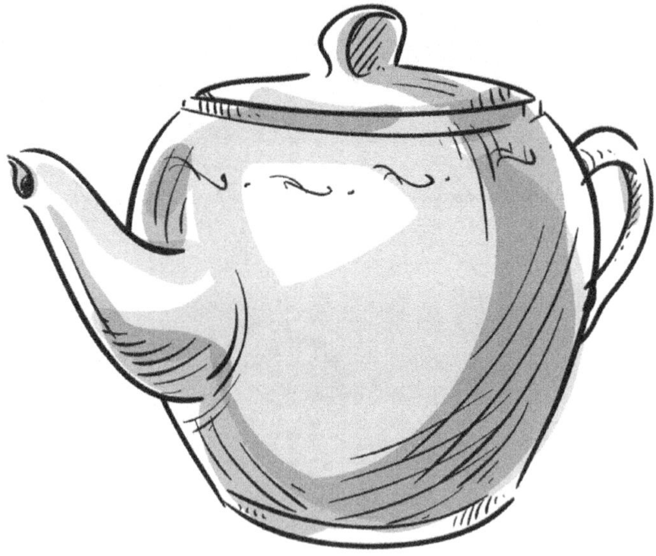

You can do this, Honey. You can do it.

I hear you wondering if it will be enough, and if you will be enough.

And I say that you are.

You have more than enough time.

More than enough energy, more than enough creativity, more than enough leadership skills.

More than enough skills...

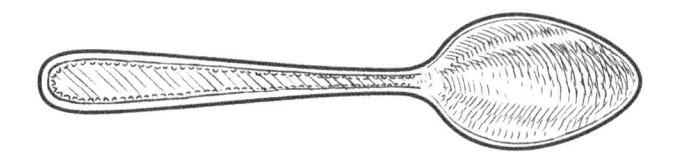

More than enough.

Give, and don't hold back today.

Give your time to your work and to Divine appointments.

Give your focus to the assignment at hand.

I'll take care of the next one, and the next, and the next.

Go into this day knowing that it is a new day.

Favor is your middle name.

And blessing follows you everywhere you go —everything you touch, everyone you encounter.

Everywhere you go, you are known as a blessing.

Remember that today.

You are a blessing, and everyone that works with you is blessed.

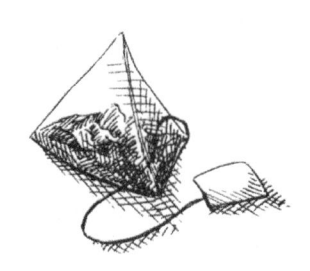

Everyone who does business with you is blessed.

Declare over them blessing because I have said it.

And know that when you approach people, you are offering them the opportunity to be blessed.

The demand for you is going to get higher and higher, and they may not even know why, but you will know.

Speak life. Declare blessing.

Everyone who works with you is blessed.

Lord, what are You saying to me today? What do You want me to hear from Your heart?

Tea Time
Truth Nugget #20

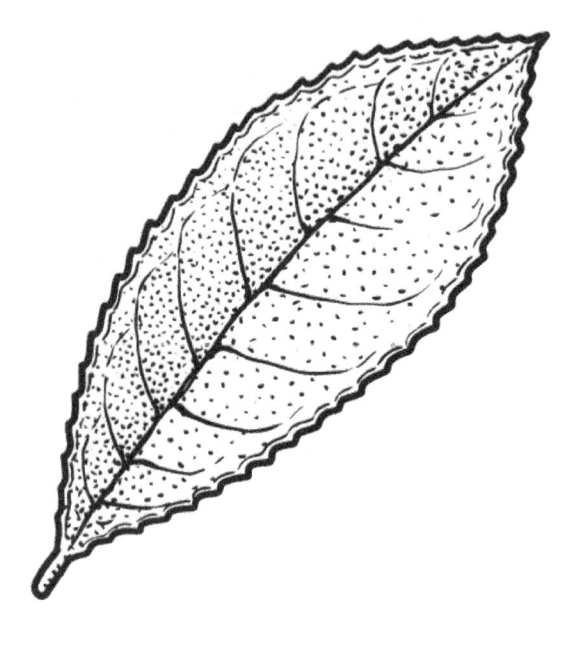

It's okay, Honey. I'm not worried.

I'm not worried by any of it.

I'm not worried about you.

I'm not worried about your business or your dreams.

I've got you. Do you hear me, Honey? I've got you.

Will you trust Me?

It's okay, let the tears flow.

This is hard.

And it's okay to say it's hard, because it is.

You are not a wimp. You need to hear that today.

You are not a wimp; you are not a failure.

The only way you can fail is if you choose it and give up.

But that's not how I designed you.

Failure is not in your DNA. or your code.

You were designed and programmed to win.

And I have you covered.

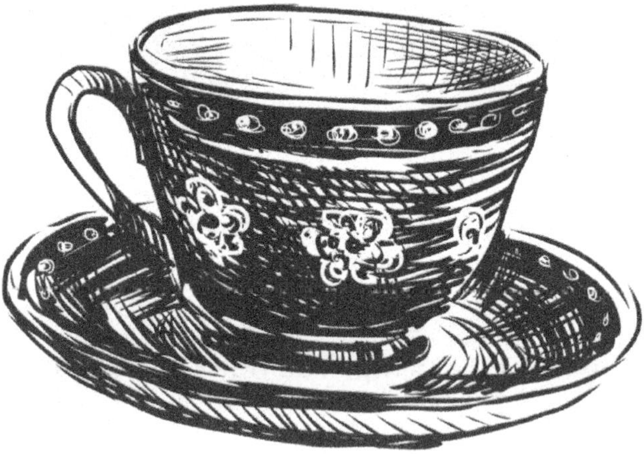

Lord, what are You saying to me today? What do You want me to hear from Your heart?

Tea Time

Truth Nugget #21

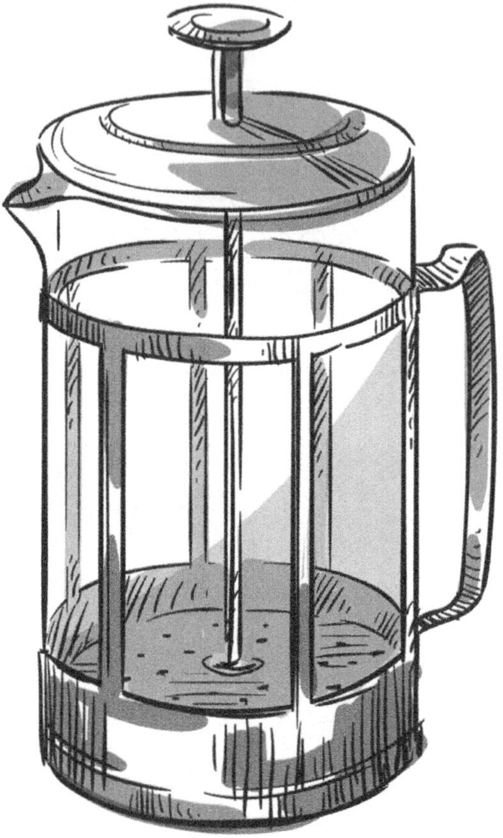

I got you.

Do you hear Me, Honey? I've got you.

And I'm not letting go.

I know this is scary. It is when you
only see half the picture.

What if I told you this was like cinematography, and what
you see is only part of the picture, a green screen.

I'm working on the special effects.

Can you trust Me that I'm not finished yet? I'm not.

This is not the end, not even close.

So don't give up on Me, Honey.

I know it's hard.

It's okay to say that.

You're not weak. You're not a wimp. You're not.

I would never, and could never, have given

this assignment to a wimp.

I placed that feisty heart inside of you
before you were born.

I knew you wouldn't quit.

And when you don't feel it, it's there. It really is. I see.

Even on the lowest of low days when you feel like you
barely have any fight left.

I still see that spark in your eyes.

So don't you quit on Me now. Honey.

This is only over if you quit.

And there is so much at stake, even more than you know.

Will you trust Me?

I've got you.

Let's go.

Lord, what are You saying to me today? What do You want me to hear from Your heart?

Tea Time
Truth Nugget #22

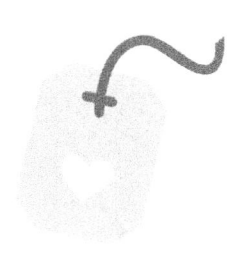

I am the author of time.

Do not fear, little flock, for it is the Father's good pleasure to give you the Kingdom.

And that includes time.

I give seed to the sower and bread to the eater.

It is time to start eating your bread.

You've been sowing it.

I'll show you when to sow and when to eat.

Trust Me with your time.

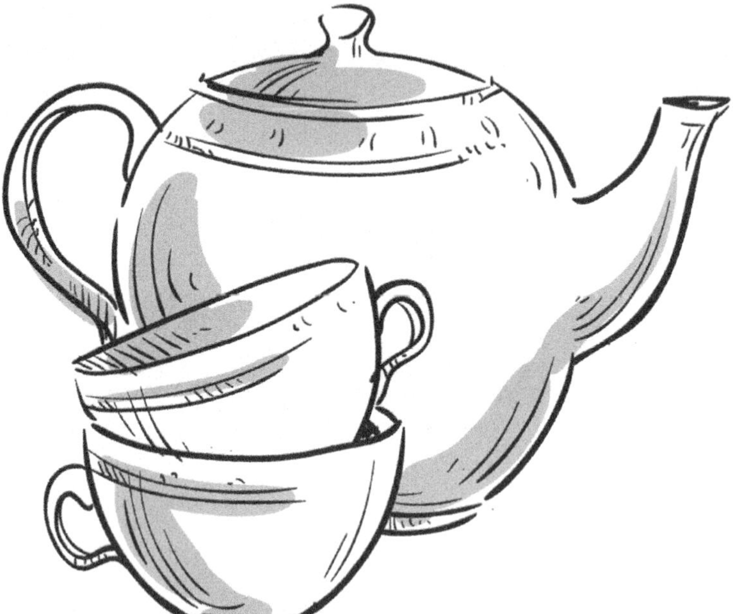

Lord, what are You saying to me today? What do You want me to hear from Your heart?

*Tea Time
Truth Nugget #23*

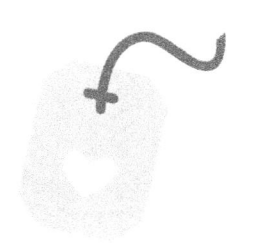

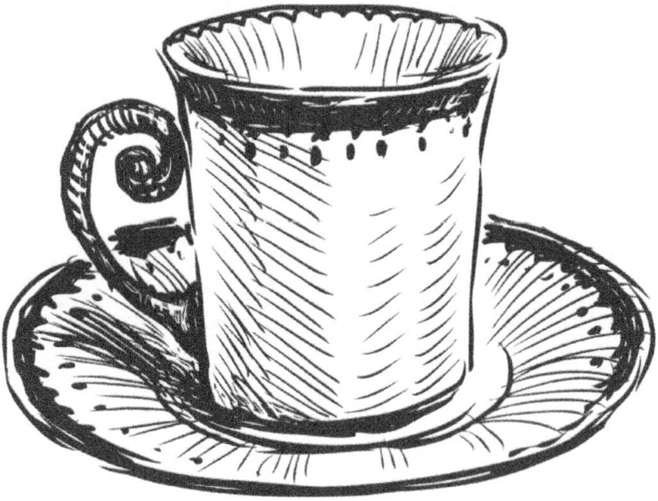

Get ready, Honey.

Get ready because you wouldn't believe it if I told you what I'm about to do.

Get ready.

Get ready to be busy and to rest.

Get ready to face things and try things that you never have before.

Get ready to grow.

Don't be afraid. You don't have to do it alone.

I am with you, and I will surround you every time with a team...every time.

Get ready, because there's going to come many opportunities that you look at and say, "I've never done this before," but I will show you how.

And at the end of the year, you're going to look back on all We've done and say, "Wow, We did that!"

And I will smile and say,

"Yes. We did!"

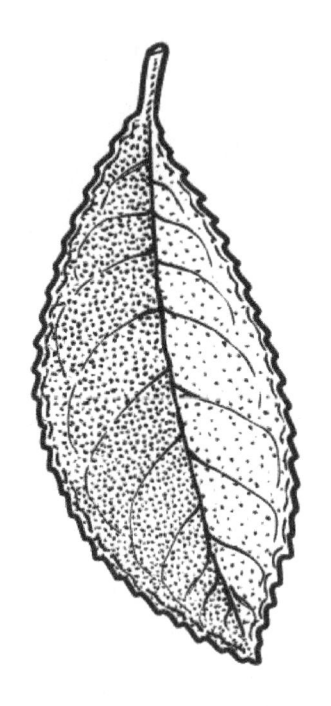

Lord, what are You saying to me today? What do You want me to hear from Your heart?

Tea Time

Truth Nugget #24

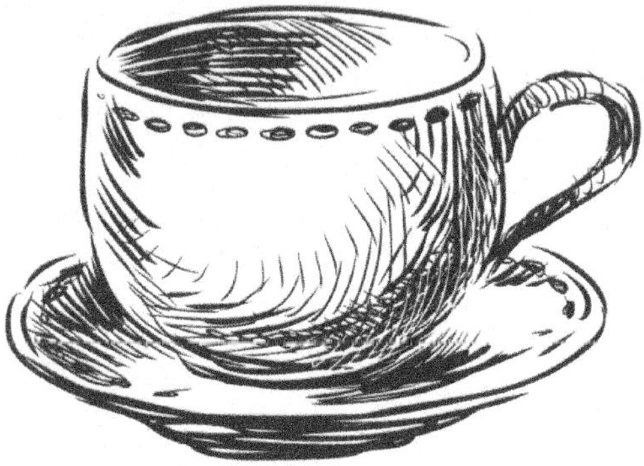

I need you to trust Me.

I need you to trust that I know where I'm taking you and what I am doing.

I need you to trust that I am enough.

and you are too.

I need you to trust those around you.

Not everyone, I'll show you who.

For right now, I need you to trust Me.

The enemy wants to cripple you with insecurity, intimidation, and second-guessing.

He can't stop you from getting there; he knows that now.

So he wants to slow you from getting there - through doubt, fear, and insecurity.

And that fear - which creates doubt - hampers creativity, and so you procrastinate.

Don't let the enemy steal your time, Honey.

Not this time.

This is a year of bold decisions.

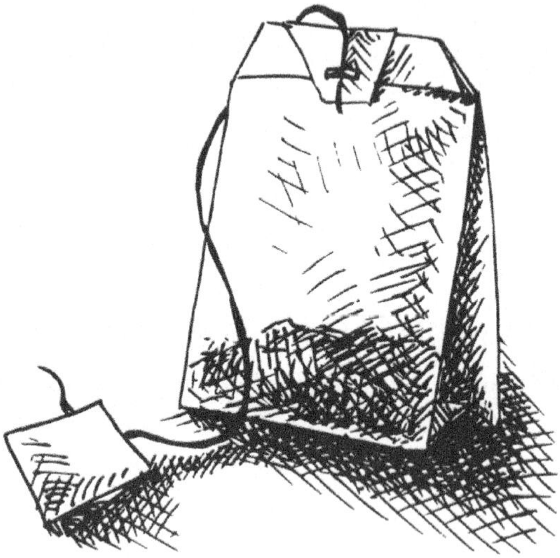

Lord, what are You saying to me today? What do You want me to hear from Your heart?

Tea Time

Truth Nugget #25

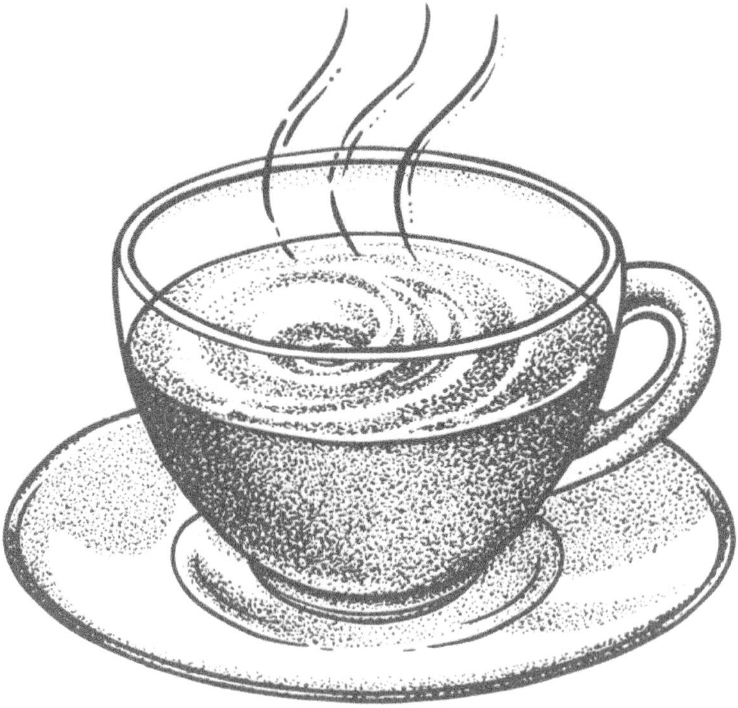

Put the outfit on and wear it.

Make a decision and go for it.

I am with you.

I am in support of you.

Consider a field...and buy it.

I am your wisdom. Not I will be, I am.

Be you.

Don't apologize for who I've made you.

Be bold. Be intentional. Be decisive.

Know that I am with you.

Say yes to things that scare you.

It's okay. I'm not scared.

Be boldly confident and trust Me.

And get ready.

Get your home ready, get your heart ready, get yourself ready, even get your wardrobe ready - because we are about to hit the ground running.

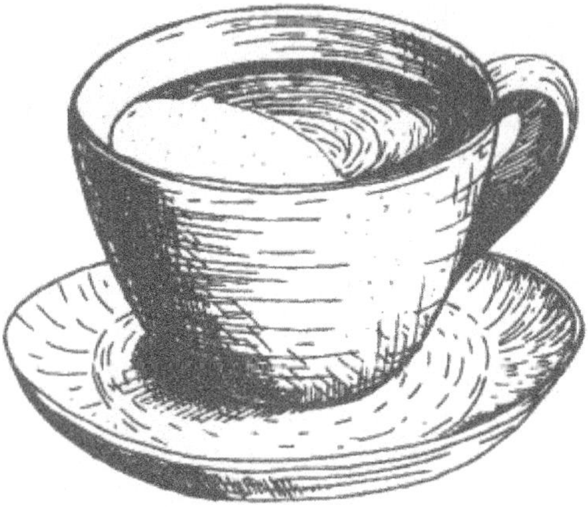

Lord, what are You saying to me today? What do You want me to hear from Your heart?

Tea Time

Truth Nugget #26

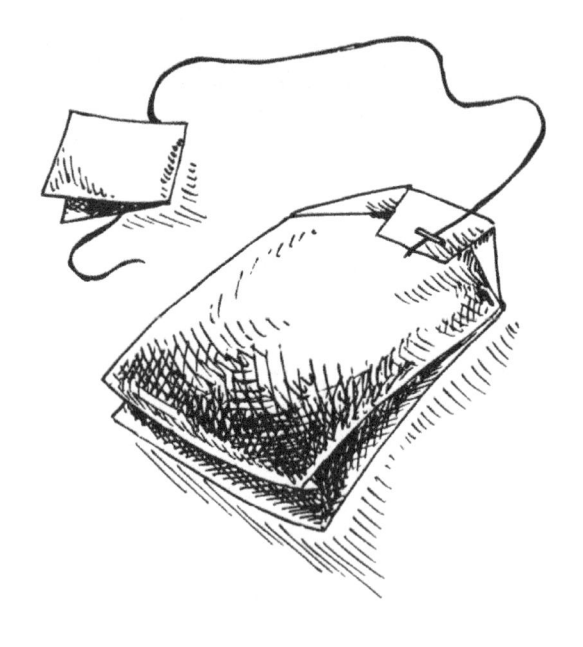

I want you to ask me bold things.

Think of yourself like Esther, but more.

She got "even up to half the kingdom."

I have given you all.

You have the ear of the King, and you have the heart of the King.

Don't be afraid.

Don't be timid; you can trust Me.

I want you to ask. Ask and be bold.

This is a year of boldness. No more intimidation and no more apologizing.

I'm going to keep saying it...be bold.

It is okay to walk in like you own the place – you do.

Let go of the little stuff, the "what if's," and the overanalyzing.

I give you permission to be who you are.

You have the ear of the King. You have the eye of the King, and I am with you.

I am in support of you.

You've been waiting for approval, for someone else to give you permission, or approve your decisions, or give you permission to decide.

That is all over now.

You are mistress of Pemberley and far more.

I give you permission, and I authorize you to decide.

It's okay, I've got you. I'm not going to let you go off course.

Let go of the carriage and pick up the reins. You can do this.

Be who I made you. I trust you.

It's time for you to trust you, too.

Don't be scared.

Be you. Be bold.

Lord, what are You saying to me today? What do You want me to hear from Your heart?

Tea Time

Truth Nugget #27

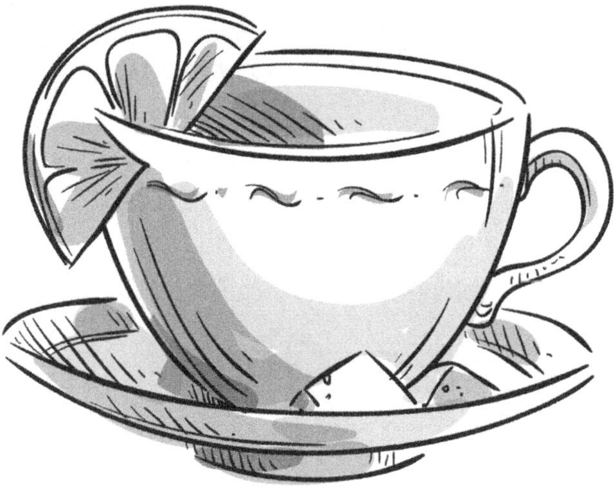

It is a new day, Honey, a new season.

Do not be afraid.

Ask, and don't hold back.

Go for it, and don't hold back.

Get an idea, run with it, and see where it takes you.

This is the year to be bold.

I give you, and I'm going to keep saying it, permission to make bold decisions.

I am with you.

I am in agreement with you

It's time to step over yesterday, step beyond the "what if's," and "are you sure," and just do it.

Go for it. Dive in feet first, so you can run.

I want you to search your heart. What do you really want?

Ask boldly, not just for others, but for yourself.

It is okay to ask. I want you to.

It's not selfish.

It is pivotal to you moving into the next season I have for you.

What is it you want?

Don't apologize for it or second guess it. Ask.

I am in agreement with you.

Lord, what are You saying to me today? What do You want me to hear from Your heart?

Tea Time

Truth Nugget #28

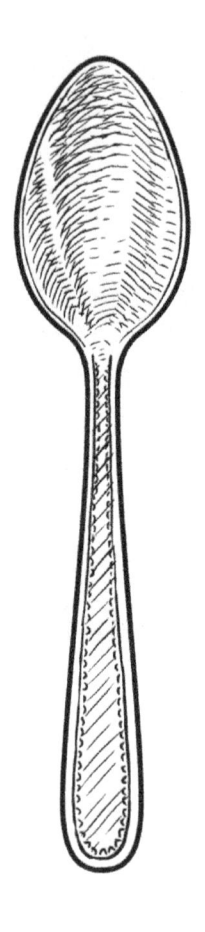

Rest.

Rest. Honey.

It's the missing ingredient from your day and without it, you won't survive.

Remember, I said it's going to get busy.

You ain't seen nothing yet!

Ask Me.

Get intentional about rest and asking Me for those windows.

I will give them to you, and I will show you.

But ask, and then keep your ears open, because they might come when you least expect it.

Look for them; seize them.

And when opportunities come,

don't wait – decide.

The longer you wait, the more it will weigh on your mind and emotions.

So don't wait, decide, and be bold in your decisions...

all your decisions.

Rest. That is your secret

weapon.

Don't overthink it, decide and move on.

It is time to get unfrozen from

the land of indecision.

Don't be afraid to decide.

Make a decision and rest.

Lord, what are You saying to me today? What do You want me to hear from Your heart?

Tea Time

Truth Nugget #29

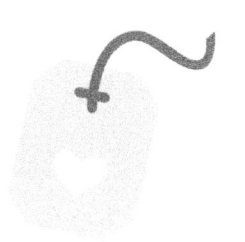

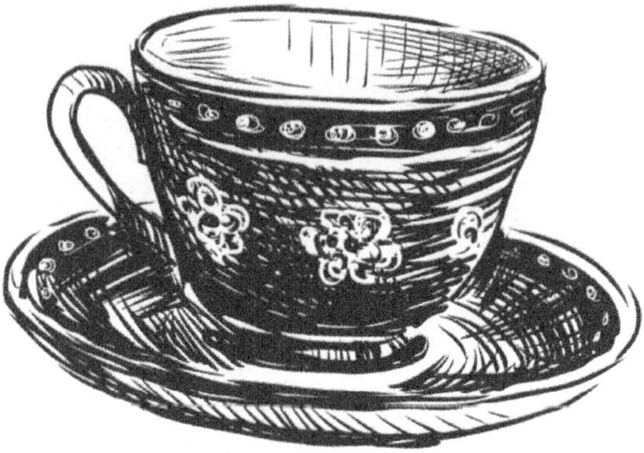

Keep thoughts on a short leash.

When you feel your emotions being rocked, look for that.

Look for the subterfuge.

What is really happening here?

What are these emotions keeping me from doing?

Uncover a plot, and you will thwart it every time.

Don't let it fester.

Assess it. Uncover it.

Dismantle it – and move on.

Move forward.

Always forward.

It is going to be a good day.

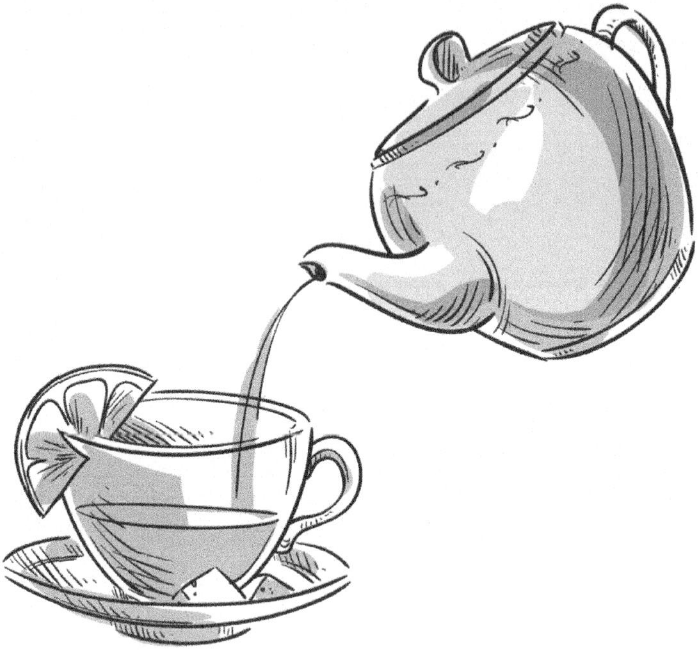

Lord, what are You saying to me today? What do You want me to hear from Your heart?

Tea Time

Truth Nugget #30

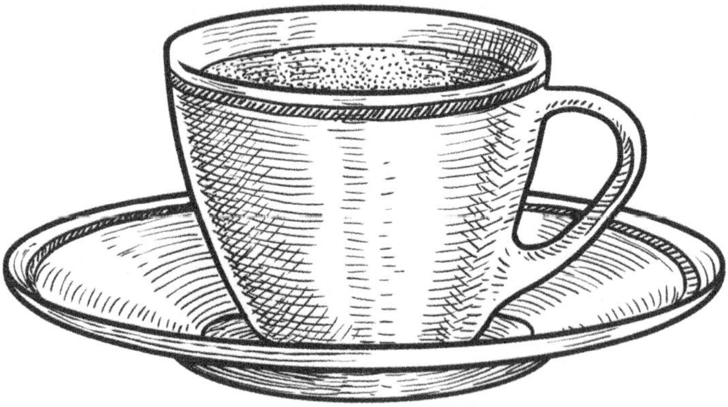

"Commit your way to the Lord. Trust also in Him, and He shall bring it to pass. He shall bring forth your righteousness as the light and your justice as the noon day. Rest in the Lord and wait patiently for Him. Do not fret. It only causes harm." Psalm 37: 5-8

Rest in Me today, Honey.

Rest in Me.

There have been many things vying for your time and attention, and there will be, but it's okay to set those aside sometimes too.

Don't let the tyranny of the urgent keep you from what is actually important.

Distractions, even good ones, split your focus and dilute your creativity - as well as your mental energy - leaving you exhausted, when all you've done is chase your tail.

Follow My lead...

Not your phone, not your "shoulds," but My lead.

I want to give you time to rest, and that's My prerogative.

I've got the details.

Trust Me with the projects that are making you scratch your head or are leaving you depleted.

I'm not depleted, I'm not out of ideas, and I know how to accomplish them all.

If I can keep the earth spinning and the planets in motion, I can handle this.

Take a deep breath, and trust Me.

Lord, what are You saying to me today? What do You want me to hear from Your heart?

*Tea Time
Truth Nugget #31*

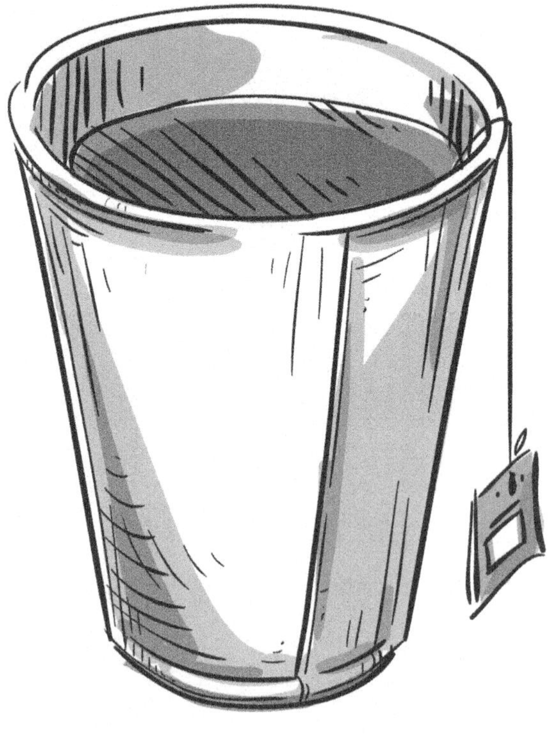

Good morning, Honey!

Today is your day!

Your mountain is waiting, so get on your way!

You're nervous, I know, but great things are in store, and I've made you ready!

So tell those nerves, "No more!"

You're gonna be great. It's gonna be good. And I'll be there with you, just like you knew I would.

Sip your tea. Leave the outcome to Me, and walk into today most confidently.

The One who has given you this sling and this stone will ever be with you; you're never alone.

Your heroes of faith are cheering you on, saying, "Keep going! No matter how long."

You've got this; I know it, and you know it, too.

And I am so very, very proud of you.

So let's get ready. Now get on your way.

Your mountain is waiting,

and today is your day![1]

---

[1] (Geisel, 1990)

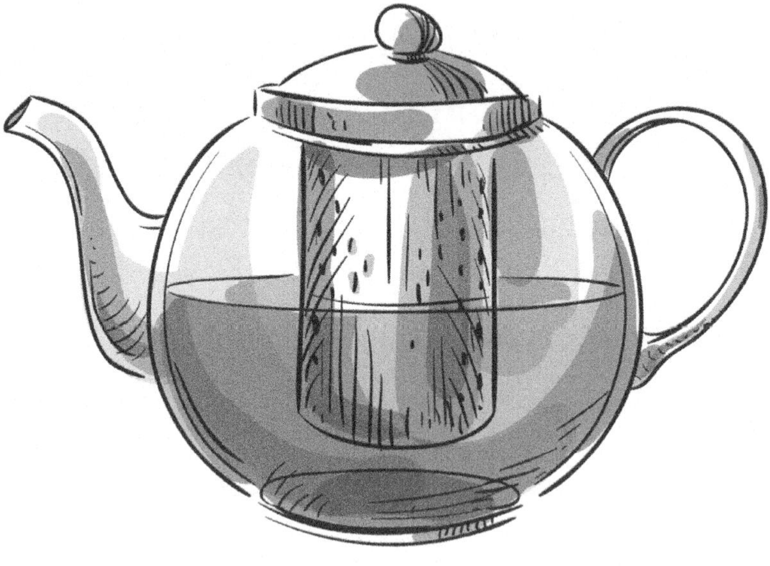

Lord, what are You saying to me today? What do You want me to hear from Your heart?

About the Author

Hello! I'm Rachel.

I'm a CEO. An entrepreneur. A public speaker. An author. A podcast host. An adventurer. A foodie. A very proud aunt. And I'm a woman on this incredible journey of business - like you.

Jesus is my best friend and has been since I was a little girl, and life with Him is my favorite adventure.

Professionally, my off-the-beaten-path career journey of twenty-two plus years has spanned multiple roles in various countries, four cities, and three states—including professional ballet, management, event production, business strategy, national and international public relations, graphic design, and marketing.

I've had the honor of serving organizations of all sizes and industries around the world to rock their brands (like a boss!) through brand strategy, brand development, content strategy, marketing strategy & execution, and user experience.

I am the owner and Chief Brand Boss of The Brand Boss Studio, host of The Brand Boss Show podcast and YouTube channel, and an in-demand public speaker. I wouldn't trade this adventure of business with Him for the world.

Before the day begins, you can find me curled up on my couch, journal in hand, enjoying Morning Tea.

More on Morning Tea

Thank you so much for reading Morning Tea, Volume 1.

I pray that the journey and journal contained in these pages have been a blessing to you!

If this book has impacted you, I'd love to hear about it.

You can connect with me directly on Instagram at @teatimetruthnuggets or send me an email at hello@teatimetruthnuggets.com. For more Morning Tea goodness, join the Morning Tea community at facebook.com/groups/morningtea.

And stay tuned for Volume 2... coming soon!

Additional Resources

🖥	Website	teatimetruthnuggets.com
f	Facebook	facebook.com/groups/morningtea
📷	Instagram	@teatimetruthnuggets
🎙	Podcast	Coming soon! Stay tuned!

Connect with Rachel

🖥	Website	brandbossstudio.com
📷	Instagram	@thebrandbossshow
in	LinkedIn	linkedin.com/in/thebrandboss

Made in the USA
Monee, IL
01 September 2021